better together*

* **This book is best read together, grownup and kid.**

 **akidsco.com**

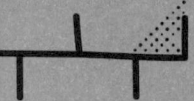

a kids book about

a kids book about

PERSEVERANCE

by Yonina Schnall Lermer

A Kids Co.
Editor Emma Wolf
Designer Rick DeLucco
Creative Director Rick DeLucco
Studio Manager Kenya Feldes
Sales Director Melanie Wilkins
Head of Books Jennifer Goldstein
CEO and Founder Jelani Memory

DK
Senior Production Editor Jennifer Murray
Senior Production Controller Louise Minihane
Senior Acquisitions Editor Katy Flint
Acquisitions Project Editor Sara Forster
Managing Art Editor Vicky Short
Managing Director, Licensing Mark Searle

First American edition, 2025
Published in the United States by DK Publishing, 1745 Broadway, 20th Floor,
New York, NY 10019

First published in Great Britain in 2025 by
Dorling Kindersley Limited, 20 Vauxhall Bridge Road, London SW1V 2SA
A Penguin Random House Company

The authorised representative in the EEA is
Dorling Kindersley Verlag GmbH. Arnulfstr. 124, 80636 Munich, Germany

A catalog record for this book is available from the Library of Congress.
A CIP catalogue record for this book is available from the British Library.
ISBN: 978-0-2417-4305-8

DK books are available at special discounts when purchased in bulk for sales
promotions, premiums, fund-raising, or education use. For details, contact:
DK Publishing Special Markets, 1745 Broadway, 20th Floor, New York, NY 10019
SpecialSales@dk.com

Printed and bound in China
www.dk.com
akidsco.com

This book was made with Forest
Stewardship Council™ certified
paper — one small step in DK's
commitment to a sustainable future.
Learn more at **www.dk.com/uk/
information/sustainability**

To my mother and father:
There are no words.

To my 3 little warriors:
We will always persevere.

Intro
for grownups

"Can you help me?", "I don't know what to do!", "This is too hard!". These became daily conversations at school with my students and at home with my kids. And one day, I had enough.

Why? Why did they seem so helpless? Why did they give up so soon?

I knew I had to begin teaching more than just the curriculum. I had to teach a skill that went beyond the classroom walls. How would these kids become successful grownups without practicing perseverance in their childhood?

Perseverance means continued effort to achieve a goal, despite challenges and obstacles.

And that's what this book is about.

It won't be easy, and it will take time and patience. But learning it together will change mindsets for both kids and grownups.

So let's get started!

YOU KNOW WHAT'S EASY?

Having someone do hard
things for you is easy.

It's easy to have someone
else tie your shoes.

It's easy to have someone
else fold a piece of paper
into an airplane for you.

YOU KNOW WHY WE LIKE THAT?

Because when it's hard,
we get frustrated.

Not a fun feeling.

When that shoe won't tie,
or the paper airplane won't fly,
we get annoyed with ourselves.

HAVE YOU EVER FELT THAT WAY?

I know I have. Sometimes,
it gets so bad that I get angry.
How come I just can't do it?
How come I just can't get it?

But one day, I learned something
incredible. I learned a word that
changed it all for me.

A TEENY-TINY WORD WITH

HUGE
POWERS!!!

That word is...

YET.

You see, when we add the word **YET,** we change our frustrations into...

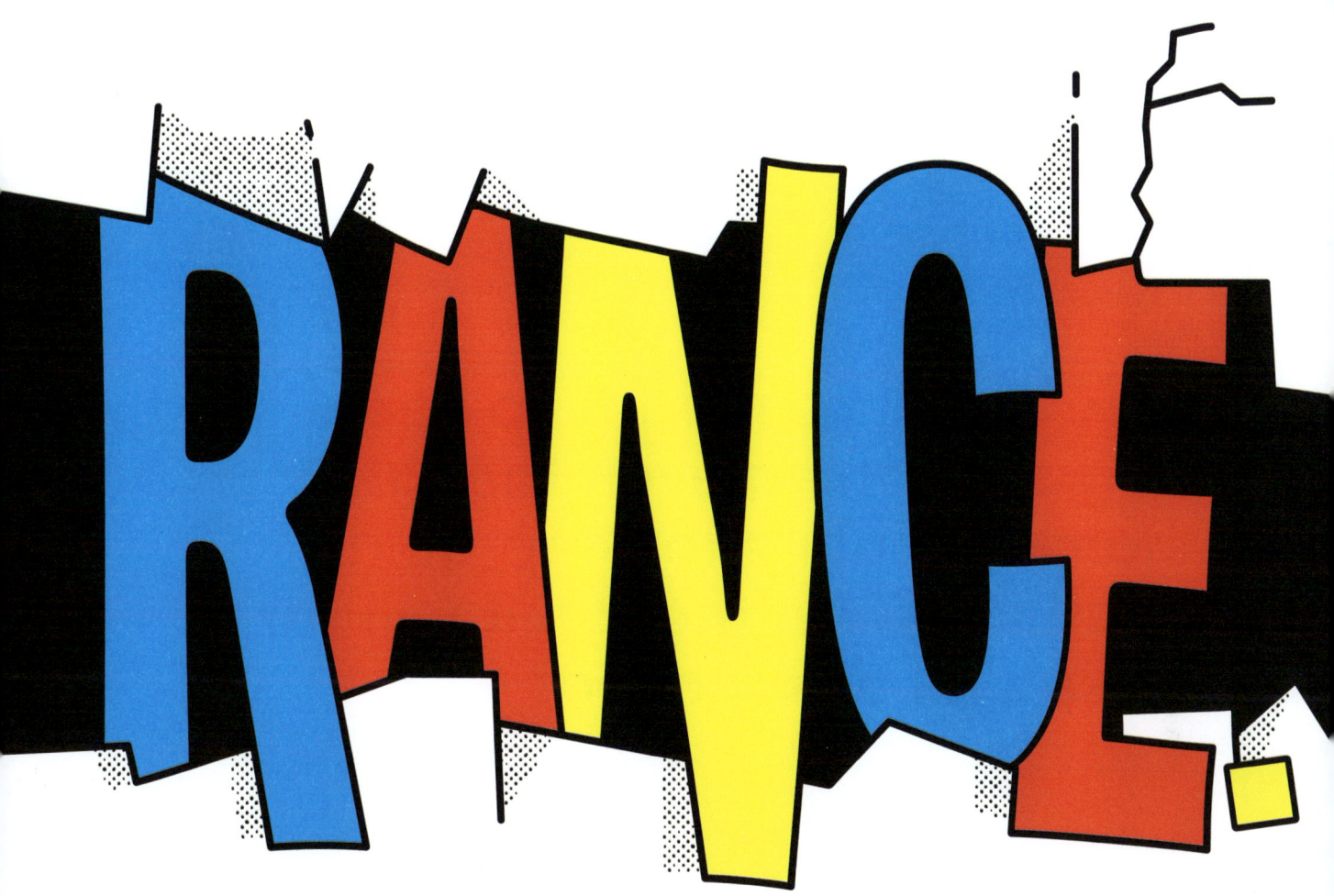

Perseverance means to keep doing something even though it is hard. It means to keep doing something even though it will take a long time to succeed.

I DON'T UNDERSTAND THIS... YET.

Did you hear that? It sounded like I was about to give up. But then I added that little word. And now, I am declaring that I will figure it out.

Let's try another one.

I DON'T KNOW HOW TO DO THIS... YET.

Wow! Did you catch that?
It sounded like I was announcing
something I just don't know how to
do. But add that word and now,
the meaning has changed.

While today I don't have the skills or
knowledge to do it, I will one day.

And boy oh boy, when that
day comes, it will feel so good.

You see, doing hard things is good for us. Just like exercising builds our muscles, learning new things helps to build our brains!

They start to grow and stretch as they fill up with all the new things we thought we couldn't do but now can!

When we keep up at doing
difficult things, we also build

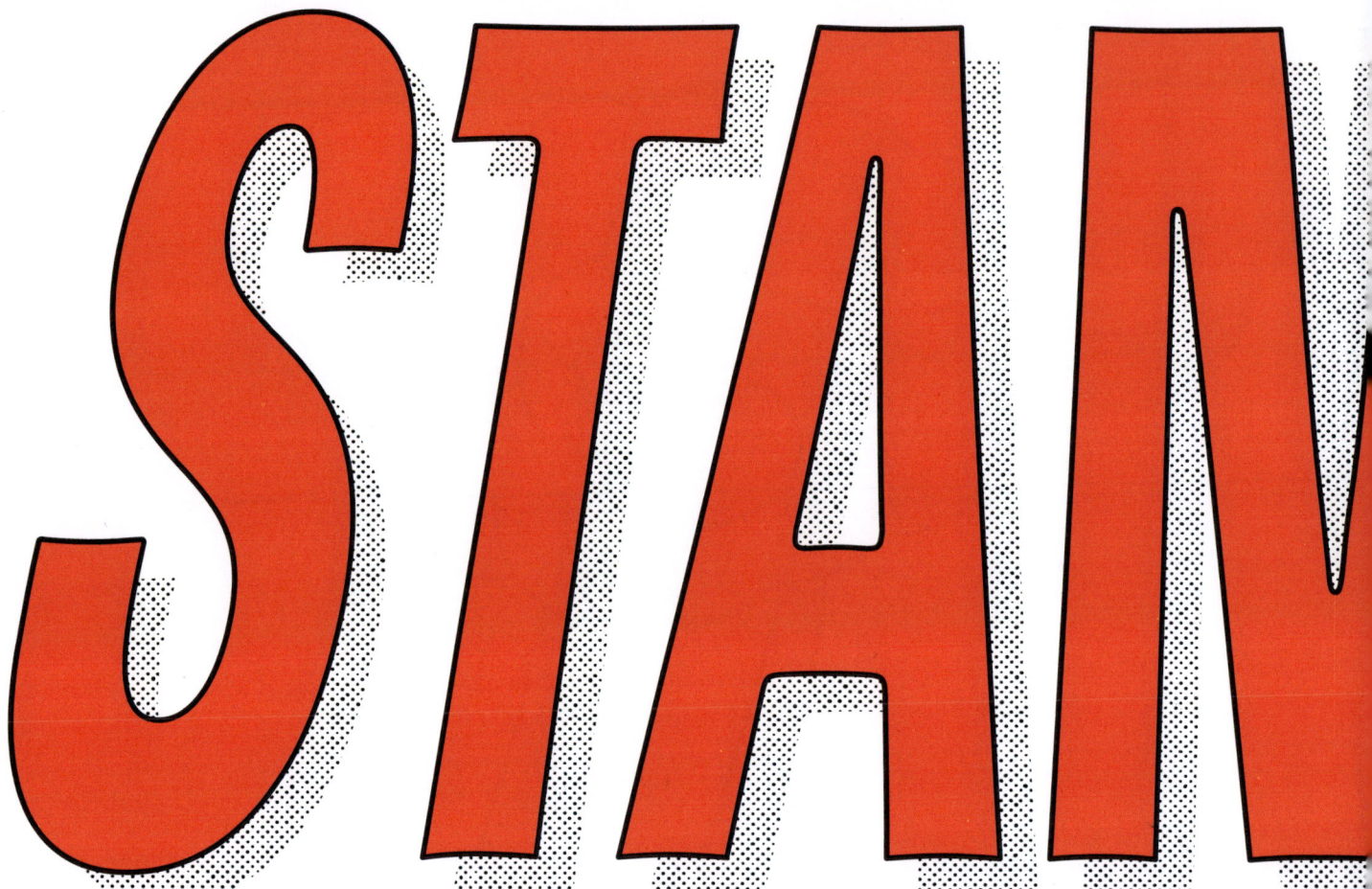

Stamina is when our minds
and bodies are able to do hard
things for a long period of time.

The more we practice those hard things,
the more we can do them.

And the more we do them,
the more comfortable we get
with feeling uncomfortable.

THAT SOUNDS FUNNY, DOESN'T IT?

Remember the frustrating feelings we talked about before? Naturally, we try our best to get rid of those feelings as fast as we can because they don't feel great.

But the power of

YET

wants those feelings to stay.

The power of **YET** wants us
to get used to those feelings.
Those feelings push us to keep
trying to achieve our goals.

If we give up immediately,
it'll never happen.

Now, don't get me wrong. We will make many mistakes on the way to **YET.** But those mistakes help us learn and realize what to do differently next time.

HOW TO SUCCEED NEXT TIME. HOW TO FINALLY REACH THE YET.

Or...will you?

Do we always reach the **YET?**

Effort doesn't always equal success. What do I mean by that?

We can work hard.
We can build stamina.
We can persevere.
And we still might not
achieve that goal.

But that doesn't mean
we're back at zero.

You see, a sneaky thing
happens on our journey to **YET.**

We **MEET** new people.

We **LEARN** about ourselves.

We **DISCOVER** new things we maybe didn't know we could do.

We **COLLECT** all sorts of mistakes and grow from them.

And even though the effort didn't bring success, we walk away with new tools to use for next time.

And here's another cool word for you...

PIVOT.

When we find ourselves standing there without the success we wanted, we don't turn around and walk back to the starting line.

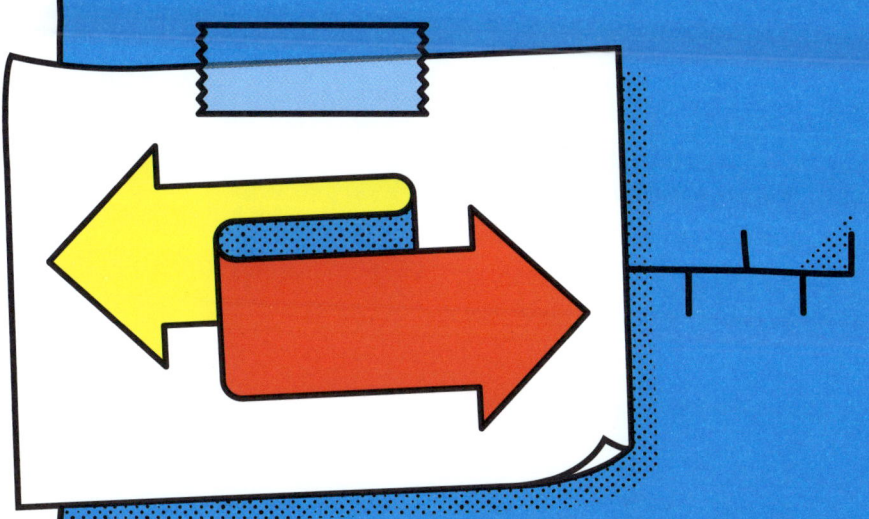

We look to the left. We look to the right. And we see where we can take those tools to start something new.

Don't go back to the beginning! That would be so silly! You've already worked so hard.

LET SUCCESS

Let's say you want to try out for the basketball team at your school.

You've decided to practice several times a week for months before the tryouts. You work to be as strong and fast as you can be!

Some days, you even play until it's dark outside, after you've already spent a whole day in school.

The tryouts come, and...
you don't make it.

Does that mean you stop playing basketball? Absolutely not!

IT'S TIME TO FIND A DIFFERENT WAY TO PLAY.

I wonder...is there another team you could try out for? Could you teach basketball to other kids? How could you use the skills you've worked hard for to make new basketball goals?

And while you're doing that, you're getting stronger, faster, and more talented at the game you already love so much.

See? We can change
what success looks like.

SO MAKE MISTAKES!
BE PROUD OF MISTAKES!
BUILD STAMINA!
AND ALLOW YOURSELF TO
PIVOT!

THE POWER OF YET.

Just a 3-letter word.

Try it today.

Use it.

And get back to me.

I can't wait to hear
what you can't do,

don't understand,

don't know,

haven't tried,

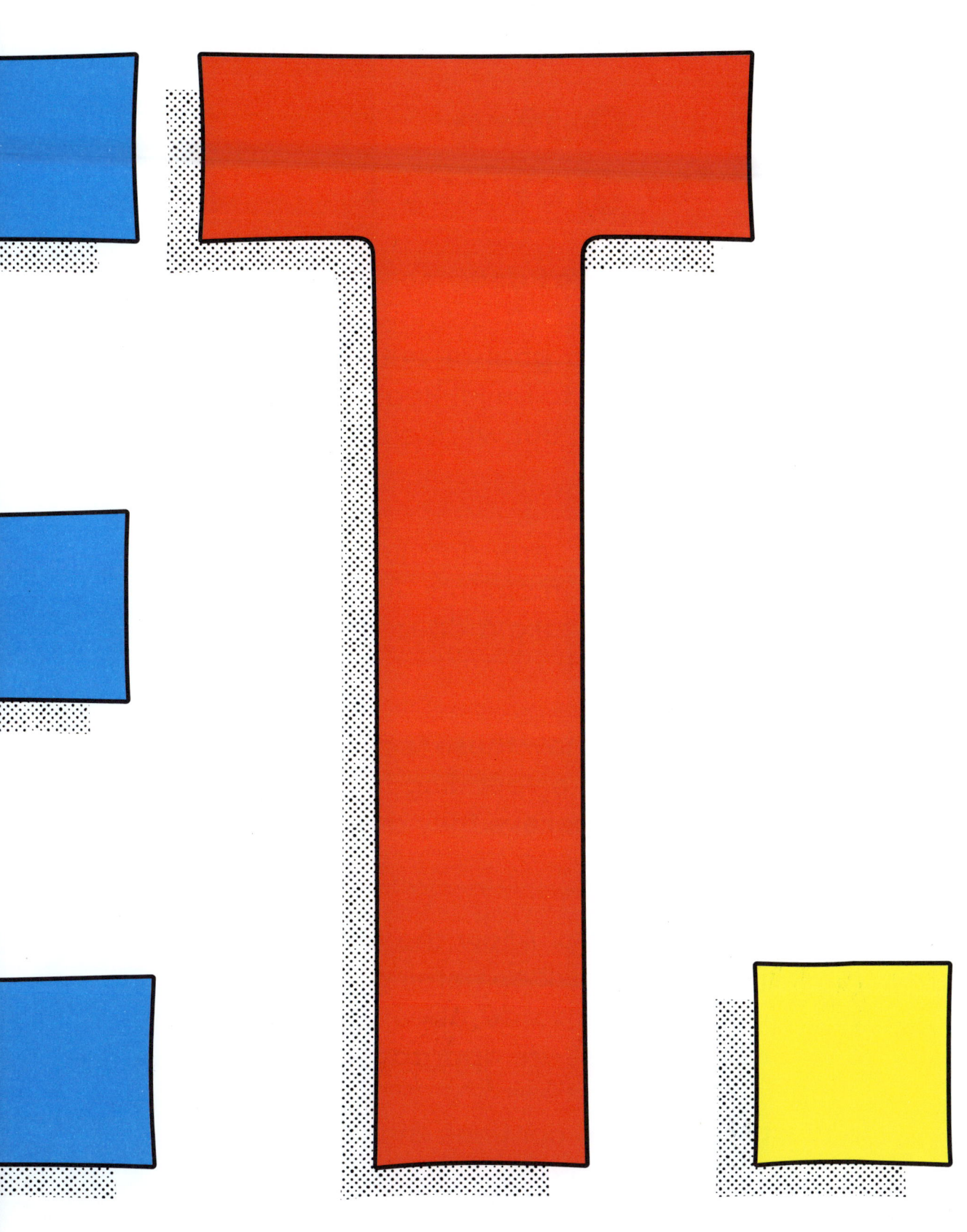

Outro
for grownups

The **Power of Yet** does more than push kids to "fail forward." It acknowledges that we want a certain goal or outcome. This kind of mindset takes time to build! Reading this book is a great place to start, but what else can you do to flex those muscles?

1. MODEL. Obstacles are not just for kids. Be transparent about moments in your own life where you need to take a deep breath, add the word "YET," or pivot!

2. VALIDATE. Let kids know these feelings are natural. You will be there as a sounding board while they find solutions. You believe they are brave enough to figure it out!

3. DON'T RUSH to help. Allow the frustration to sit for a bit. Perhaps ask something like, "What do you think you'd like to do about it?" If need be, offer strategies that are appropriate.

And most importantly, continue the conversation.

About The Author

Yonina (she/her) spends her days with kids as a teacher and mother. She noticed that instead of weighing outcomes and making decisions to solve problems, children immediately turn to grownups for solutions. When things don't work out, they simply give up. Even with day-to-day problems, kids shrug their shoulders and wait for someone else to come help. As parents and teachers, we come from a place of protection and love when we rush to their aid. However, doing so removes an opportunity for their growth. Yonina is on a mission to encourage grownups to be cheerleaders on the sidelines while helping kids through challenges.

This book was written to start that conversation. To remind kids that doing hard things is not comfortable... and that's OK.

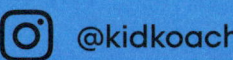 @kidkoach   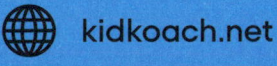 kidkoach.net

Made to empower.

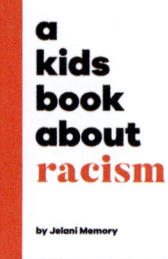

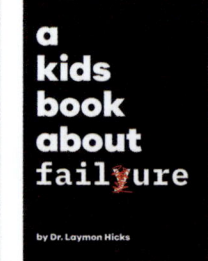

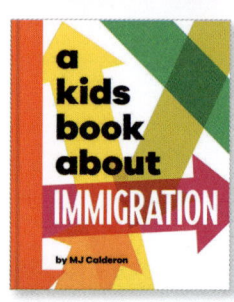

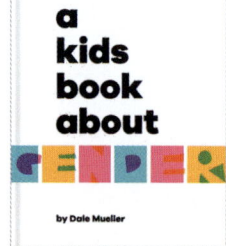
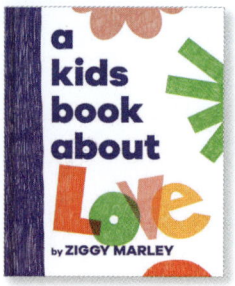
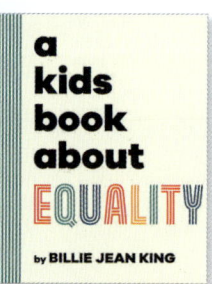

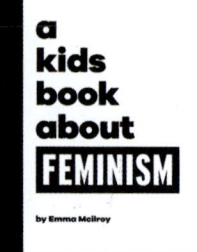

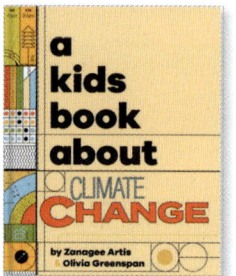

Discover more at akidsco.com